Wondering: Luke's re| the coming of Christ

T0326801

Luke 2.1-20

¹In those days a decree went out from Emperor Augustus that all the world should be registered. ²This was the first registration and was taken while Quirinius was governor of Syria. ³All went to their own towns to be registered. ⁴Joseph also went from the town of Nazareth in Galilee to Judea, to the city of David called Bethlehem, because he was descended from the house and family of David. ⁵He went to be registered with Mary, to whom he was engaged and who was expecting a child. ⁶ While they were there, the time came for her to deliver her child. ⁷And she gave birth to her firstborn son and wrapped him in bands of cloth, and laid him in a manger, because there was no place for them in the inn. ⁸ In that region there were shepherds living in the fields, keeping watch over their flock by night. ⁹Then an angel of the Lord stood before them, and the glory of the Lord shone around them, and they were terrified. ¹⁰But the angel said to them, 'Do not be afraid; for see – I am bringing you good news of great joy for all the people: ¹¹to you is born this day in the city of David a Saviour, who is the Messiah, the Lord. ¹²This will be a sign for you: you will find a child wrapped in bands of cloth and lying in a manger.' ¹³And suddenly there was with the angel a multitude of the heavenly host, praising God and saying, ¹⁴'Glory to God in the highest heaven, and on earth peace among those whom he favours!' ¹⁵When the angels had left them and gone into heaven, the shepherds said to one another, 'Let us go now to Bethlehem and see this thing that has taken place, which the Lord has made known to us.' ¹⁶So they went with haste and found Mary and Joseph, and the child lying in the manger. ¹⁷When they saw this, they made known what had been told them about this child; ¹⁸and all who heard it were amazed at what the shepherds told them. ¹⁹But Mary treasured all these words and pondered them in her heart. ²⁰The shepherds returned, glorifying and praising God for all they had heard and seen, as it had been told them.

This first session is an exploration of Luke's account of the birth of Jesus – Luke 2.1-20.

This is really a Bible Study. If you're not used to Bible Studies, don't be put off! It's surprising how much there is in the text of scripture when we start to dig into it and tease out what it has to say to us in our own situation. In doing so we'll be following in the steps of Mary, the mother of Jesus, of whom Luke reports that she 'treasured all these words and pondered them in her heart' (v.19).

> "That's the whole problem with science. You've got a bunch of empiricists trying to describe things of unimaginable wonder."
>
> Bill Watterson, cartoonist and author

So that we can all do this Bible Study together, you'll find the relevant passage set out at the start of each session, or you can use your own Bible (version NRSV). Whichever you choose, you'll find it helpful to have the text in front of you as we go along. The aim of this session is to help our pondering on the birth of Jesus – hopefully without actually becoming ponderous!

God of surprises

Luke 2.1-5: The particular focus of Luke's account of the birth of Christ is in telling the story of what happened, and letting that story speak for itself.

By giving clear statements of both time and location, his first concern is to establish that a real event took place. But more than that, Luke's whole purpose in writing his gospel is to help us discover the other side of this event – that God in Christ desires to visit us in our lives and our setting. Luke wants us to know not only that Christ became incarnate in this world, now over two thousand years ago, but that God can become known to us, incarnate in our lives today.

It's worthwhile looking at this passage in some detail, since the significance of the coming of Christ was missed by so many at the time. We, today, can just as easily miss the presence and prompting of God, unless we are looking out for Jesus' coming.

Divine humility

Luke 2.6-7: The birth of Christ is described in strikingly low-key terms. If what Luke is reporting had been offered for publication in a newspaper, he would no doubt have been sent away and told to write it up to 'make something of it'.

Yet this simplicity underlines the humanity and humility of God. The story, rightly understood, is doubly striking. That God would be willing to become a human being and share the precarious lot of humanity is amazing enough. That Jesus did this so fully that he was willing to become a vulnerable and totally dependent infant (lacking a home, let alone a hospital bed in which to be born) is quite breathtaking. Humility, we immediately see, is not about putting ourselves down: that is false humility. It is, rather, trusting

"The feeling of awed wonder that science can give us is one of the highest experiences of which the human psyche is capable. It is a deep aesthetic passion to rank with the finest that music and poetry can deliver. It is truly one of the things that make life worth living and it does so, if anything, more effectively if it convinces us that the time we have for living is quite finite."

Richard Dawkins, scientist and atheist

HOW TO GET THE MOST OUT OF THIS COURSE

SUGGESTIONS FOR GROUP MEMBERS

1. THE MATERIAL Scattered through the text are boxes containing a variety of quotes. They do not necessarily refer directly to that page – or even that session. They're there to trigger some thoughts. You can ignore them completely if you like – though some people say that they're one of the best bits!

2. PREPARATION It'll help you enormously if you're able to have your own personal copy of this booklet (so the price is reduced either when multiple copies are ordered or if you order online). Try to have read each session *before* the meeting.

3. USING A TRANSCRIPT The Transcript booklet is a complete record of the words as spoken on the CD. It may help you to feel more 'on top of' the material and give you greater confidence about joining in the discussion. Reading the transcript at leisure after the session may help you absorb the text.

SUGGESTIONS FOR GROUP LEADERS

We're deliberately not prescriptive, and different leaders prefer to work in slightly different ways, but here are a few tried and trusted ideas …

1. THE ROOM Discourage people from sitting outside or behind the main circle – it's good for all to feel equally involved.

2. HOSPITALITY Tea or coffee and biscuits on arrival and/or at the end of a meeting is always appreciated and encourages people to talk informally.

3. THE START If group members don't know each other well, some kind of 'icebreaker' might be helpful. For example, you might invite people to share something about themselves and/or about their faith. Be careful to place a time limit on this exercise!

4. PREPARING THE GROUP Explain that there are no right or wrong answers, and that among friends it is fine to say things that you are not sure about – to express half-formed ideas. If individuals choose to say nothing, that is all right too.

5. THE MATERIAL Encourage members to read each session *before* the meeting. It helps if each group member has their own personal copy of this booklet. **There is no need to consider all the questions.** A lively exchange of views is what matters, so be selective.

6. PREPARATION Decide beforehand whether to distribute (or ask people to bring) paper, pencils, hymn books etc. If you're going to ask anyone to do anything e.g. lead prayer or read a Bible passage, do give them advance notice so they can prepare.

7. TIMING Try to start on time and make sure you stick fairly closely to your stated finishing time.

8. USING THE CD The track markers on the CD (and shown in the Transcript) will help you find your way around the CD very easily. For each of the sessions we recommend reading through the session in the course booklet, before listening together to all of the relevant session on the CD. And then tackle the Questions for Groups.

9. USING THE TRANSCRIPT The Transcript is a complete record of the words as spoken on the CD. You'll find this invaluable as you prepare. Group members will undoubtedly benefit from having a copy, if they so wish.

INTRODUCTION
LIVING IN THE LIGHT of the coming of Christ

As a child, the point of Christmas for me was to take apart my new toys and find out how they worked. I was usually able to put them back together, often with a few bits left over. The only problem was that they never really worked after that!

Modern Western culture is like that. We have been brilliant at taking things apart, right down to splitting the atom, and have produced great technological innovations as a result. But we struggle to see life as a whole, to put it back together again. That could be why spirituality is so in fashion. We will have heard someone we know, or some well-known person, say something like, 'I'm not religious but I am a spiritual person'. It sounds attractive, but it is not easy to know quite what it means.

Spirituality has been defined as 'how I make sense of life'. For many of us life is busy, complex and fragmented. There is a desire, a longing, to make sense of it. Alan Bennett, in a wonderful take-off of a sermon, said, in a very parsonical voice: *'Life is like a sardine tin, everyone is looking for the key'*! Instinctively, we try to make sense of life, to 'find ourselves' and our part in this wonderful, yet deeply flawed, humanity to which we belong.

Christian spirituality has much to contribute to this search. It has a number of distinctive characteristics. It has been tested in a vast range of different settings for over two thousand years and has stood the test of time. Its starting point is not the self, but the otherness of God. It is, essentially, a response to something outside of ourselves – someone beyond us. Its focus is not on how we can get control of our lives, though it does that wonderfully well. Rather, its focus is on letting go, trusting ourselves to the goodness, nearness and guidance of God.

This course looks at the response of four people living at or around the time of the birth of Jesus to that amazing event, and at its implications for us. Two of them are Gospel writers, Luke and John. The other two both had unique and striking encounters with Christ, namely, Mary the mother of Christ, and Paul the great Apostle of the Church.

In looking at their varied responses to the coming of Christ, the course identifies four elements in the practice of Christian spirituality (*wonder, pondering, receiving* and *living*) that give us a track to run on as we seek to make sense of life by living in the light of the coming of Christ.

God to hold us up and see us through whatever happens to us in life. Two people described in the Bible as 'meek' are Moses and Jesus; that is because they were devoted to God's purposes in their lives and their world – not because either of them was a 'push-over'!

> "We are perishing for want of wonder, not for want of wonders."
>
> *G K Chesterton, author*

Jesus' birth shows us how at home God is in our world. Maybe that's because it actually is God's world. The Old Testament scriptures make it clear that we're made in the image of God. We share in a finite way God's own freedom of will, capacity for moral judgement and ability to choose the way of love. We also share attributes such as the power of speech, and awareness of truth, beauty, and the capacity to wonder.

So, in the coming of Christ, we see two remarkable 'working demonstrations'. We see what God is like, for Jesus is 'the living image of his Father'. But Jesus, in living the life of a human being, shows us what it means to be a living image of God – to become fully human. It is about being open to the presence of God: reaching out in love to all, including the vulnerable and the (to us) unattractive. It is about looking to God for the wisdom and strength to discover and play our part in God's purposes of love for all creation.

God's disturbing presence

Luke 2.8-14: There now bursts into this ordinariness a most extra-ordinary happening: the coming together of two groups not known for holding joint meetings – shepherds and angels! Shepherds were considered the lowest of the low, the down-and-outs of society. Their 24/7 work schedule meant they had no time for the religious festivals and ceremonies that were considered essential for holiness. They were definitely not 'your average church-goers'!

Yet it is to them that a company of the angels is sent, to tell them just how special this 'ordinary' birth was, and to encourage them to join in the celebrations of heaven. It was, quite literally, a 'heaven-sent' invitation to a party-with-a-difference! A single angel stands before them in 'the glory of the Lord'.

'The glory of the Lord' is a term often used in the Old Testament to describe the presence of God. It is like a cloud of intense brightness, that provokes awe and wonder in those present. It is often associated with weight. When the disciples experienced this nearness of the presence of God, the 'weight' made them sleepy (Luke 9.32) and in 22.45 they 'slept for sorrow'. It is an overwhelming sense of the presence, the goodness, the glory and the

> "The Voyager 2 satellite, that went around the various planets of the solar system, and has now reached the edge of the solar system – it's been travelling at nearly a million miles a day, and it has taken 37 years to reach the edge of the solar system; and if it carries on to the nearest star it will take 44,000 years. And it just makes me marvel at the sheer size and wonder of it all."
>
> *Canon Robert Warren (on the course CD)*

greatness of God. Notice that this takes place before the angel says anything. First comes the experience of the presence of God and then comes an *interpretation* of the event.

As in so many other instances of this experience of God, the first word of the angel is one of reassurance: 'Do not be afraid' (v.10). We humans have a deep-seated fear about encountering something bigger than us – something awesome, mystical and majestic. Something outside of our control. As T S Eliot put it in *The Four Quartets*, 'Humanity cannot bear very much reality'.

Perhaps this is why we shy away from being still, and being on our own. It is why the Psalmist tells us of God's invitation to *'be still and know that I am God'*. (Psalm 46.10.) We miss so much by keeping busy and avoiding silence.

The wonder and meaning of it all

Having received a glimpse of the glory and joy of heaven, the shepherds are ready to hear details of what has been happening in lowly Bethlehem.

We readers know at least something about this birth – but the shepherds know nothing. They do not know it is the birth of Emmanuel, 'God-with-us'. The message of the angel is so succinct: *'good news of great joy for all the people'* (v.10). There are no qualifications, or 'terms and conditions', just simply good news for all. News of a God who, at great cost, brings joy, goodness, hope, glory and grace to a troubled world. The angelic choir certainly 'got the point' and burst into song.

Now comes a fuller unpacking of the significance of this birth that describes the coming of *'a Saviour, who is the Messiah, the Lord'*. These three titles encapsulate the long-held hopes of the children of Israel.

- **Saviour:** the One who will rescue us from our enemies, from poverty, oppression and bondage – including our bondage to getting our own way in life. The great German theologian, Rudolph Bultmann, defined sin simply as *'our determination to manage by ourselves'*.

- **Messiah:** is the Hebrew word for 'saviour' – the One prophesied from of old, *'great David's greater son'*, who brings the presence of God into our lives, shining light on the path to God, in both our joys and sorrows.

- **Lord:** of all that is. Yet also a just and gentle Lord of whom we are told that *'a bruised reed he will not break and a dimly burning wick he will not quench'* (Isaiah 42.3), for *'my yoke is easy and my burden is light'* (Matthew 11.30). 'Lord' was also a concept familiar to the Gentiles as the focus of their spiritual quest – as was the term 'Christ' ('the anointed one').

The final part of the angelic message draws attention to the contrast between the ordinariness of the birth and the extra-ordinariness of the angelic presence: *'you will find a child wrapped in bands of cloth and lying in a manger'* (v.12).

No sooner have the shepherds been pointed towards the child in a cattle feeding-trough than all heaven breaks out:

'And suddenly there was with the angel a multitude of the heavenly host, praising God and saying,

'Glory to God in the highest heaven, and on earth peace among those whom he favours.' (v.13,14)

For a short while the veil between heaven and earth, between this passing Age and the Age to Come, is drawn apart. Here at the First Coming we gain a glimpse of what the Second Coming will be like; and what life is already like in the presence of God.

One of the Pictish kings of ancient Britain, on being told the Christian message and encouraged to embrace the faith, asked: 'What will I find if I do so?' The reply St Brendan gave was: 'You will find wonder upon wonder and ever wonder true'. It is this that is both the source and the focus of Christian worship.

A suitable response

Luke 2.15-20: The child has been born, the angels have opened a window into heaven and a new possibility for humanity has dawned on the world. The wise men worshipped the Christ-child (Matthew 2.11). The shepherds made haste to visit the baby and to spread the news. The saints have taught us that the highest form of

> "There are some situations that perhaps an inner sense of Christ's power and peace, though there and though present, is not quite enough. And in that moment for me, God sent me someone else along just to be, if you like, an encourager for me in a very dark moment."
>
> Revd Dr Rob Frost talking on York Course *In the Wilderness*.

worship is adoration – holding ourselves in silent wonder before the presence of God.

The response of Mary and Joseph is to ponder – which is something more profound than simply thinking. They are open to be changed by the process, seeing all of life – not least their priorities and choices – in a new, life-giving light.

Mary and Joseph never came to an end of their pondering. At different stages of their lives they would find different aspects of God and God's call to them coming to the fore. Such is the adventure of faith. This is to be our experience too if we dare to stop long enough to give God our undivided, sustained and full attention.

Our response to the coming of Christ

There are many ways that Christians down the years have responded to the coming of Christ. Two aspects of Mary's response are noted by Luke:

- **Treasuring:** This is about valuing and taking delight in something or someone. It was certainly the response of the angels. They saw the wonder and the good news *'of great joy for all the people'* (v.11), and were caught up in that joy. This is what we all need to do: to give time – personally and corporately – to be attentive to, and take unhurried delight in, the coming of Christ. How easily time spent delighting in God gets squeezed out by our supposedly busy lives. In public worship the danger for many of us is simply that we have been coming for so long that we have forgotten why we come – namely to pay loving attention to God.

- **Pondering:** Pondering is like looking at a beautiful scene, a work of art or listening to wonderful music and singing. Such experiences hold our full attention, touching not just our emotions but our soul. It affects who we are, how we see life and what we value in it. In response we hold ourselves in stillness before the object of our wonder. As we do this wondering we discover fresh insights and new depths to what has gained our attention.

Meditating on the scriptures is one of the most enduring ways in which Christians have reflected on the coming of Christ. This involves reading the scriptures, being still before them and allowing them to show us more of the nature and goodness of God. We then respond with praise, thanksgiving and silent adoration. It leads to a change in our priorities in life and to our welcoming the coming of Christ into every aspect of our living.

> "Wonder is the basis of worship."
>
> *Thomas Carlyle (1795-1881),*
> *philosopher and essayist*

QUESTIONS FOR GROUPS

1. Some people find the thought of a 'Bible study' unfamiliar and even daunting. Others have positive experiences of studying the Bible in a group. What do you think you will find most difficult or most stimulating about doing this? (You might like to keep a note of your answers so you can refer back to them at the end of the course.)

2. **Re-visit track 4 of the CD/Transcript.** People often say 'I am not religious but I am spiritual'. What do you think they mean?

3. **On track 5 of the CD/Transcript** Robert says, 'For the Christian, spirituality is about how we relate to God and how we allow God to have some say in the way that we handle our lives.' Does this describe your own experience?

4. Read Richard Dawkins' words in the box at the foot of p. 4. Are you happy with what he says?

5. A recent HM Revenue and Customs advertisement reads: 'Do your Tax Return early and find inner peace.' What does that tell us about society's approach to spirituality today?

6. The angels, shepherds and Mary were all, in their different ways, struck by the wonder of the coming of Christ. What strikes you most about the wonder of the coming of Christ?

7. Read Rob Frost's words in the box on p. 7. 'God moves in mysterious ways, his wonders to perform' says the hymn. Can you give an example from your own life?

8. Has anything given you a sense of wonder? Perhaps the delight in something small yet perfect, or being over-awed by something majestic? **Track 7 of the CD/Transcript.**

9. **Track 11 on the CD/Transcript.** Can you share any ways in which seeking to follow Christ has affected your approach to life?

10. Robert writes on p. 4. 'Humility ... is not about putting ourselves down: that is false humility'. Where are you in the humility stakes? **Track 12 on the CD/transcript may help.**

Pondering: John's reflections on the coming of Christ

John 1.1-18

¹*In the beginning was the Word, and the Word was with God, and the Word was God. ²He was in the beginning with God. ³All things came into being through him, and without him not one thing came into being. What has come into being ⁴in him was life, and the life was the light of all people. ⁵The light shines in the darkness, and the darkness did not overcome it.⁶ There was a man sent from God, whose name was John. ⁷He came as a witness to testify to the light, so that all might believe through him. ⁸He himself was not the light, but he came to testify to the light. ⁹The true light, which enlightens everyone, was coming into the world. ¹⁰He was in the world, and the world came into being through him; yet the world did not know him. ¹¹He came to what was his own, and his own people did not accept him. ¹²But to all who received him, who believed in his name, he gave power to become children of God, ¹³who were born, not of blood or of the will of the flesh or of the will of man, but of God. ¹⁴And the Word became flesh and lived among us, and we have seen his glory, the glory as of a father's only son, full of grace and truth. ¹⁵(John testified to him and cried out, 'This was he of whom I said, "He who comes after me ranks ahead of me because he was before me."') ¹⁶From his fullness we have all received, grace upon grace. ¹⁷The law indeed was given through Moses; grace and truth came through Jesus Christ. ¹⁸No one has ever seen God. It is God the only Son, who is close to the Father's heart, who has made him known.*

Pondering something usually results in understanding the significance of that subject.

Luke's report of the birth of Christ left us with Mary 'pondering all these things in her heart'. John picks up this pondering in his own particular setting. By the time he wrote his gospel, most believers came from a Greek rather than Jewish background. John has clearly engaged in deep reflection – not least about how to tell the good news of Jesus Christ in this new setting.

This is always the task of Christians and the Christian church: to find ways to speak into our particular situations. We are not called to proclaim the gospel again, but to proclaim it afresh – wherever we find ourselves. One of the most vital and effective ways we do that is by living in the light of the coming of Jesus. As has been said:

'Many will never read the gospel according to Matthew, Mark, Luke or John, but they will read the gospel according to you!'

> "The pondering heart is a thankful heart."
> *Todd Stocker, American pastor and writer*

Seeing the glory of God

John 1.1-3: Mark's gospel began with an account of the ministry of John the Baptist. Matthew began by tracing Christ's family tree back to Abraham, the great 'father of the faith' through whom God promises that all nations would be blessed. Luke goes yet further back, tracing Christ's family back to Adam – an idea amplified by Paul as he identifies Jesus as the Second Adam – the first born of a new humanity living with a personal awareness of God (Romans 5.12-21).

John now takes us even further back, introducing his gospel with the opening words of the whole Bible: 'in the beginning'. Here we are right at the start of creation. But notice, Christ is not the first created being, rather he was with God in the very work of bringing all that is into being: 'all things came into being through him' (v.3).

> "He [St John] was writing 30, 40 years after … the first three Gospels. He would have had them; he would have seen them and the story has been told – but what he is giving us is the wonderful gift of his pondering on what was happening. So here is the Christmas story from what you might call a 'pondering' perspective."
>
> *Canon Robert Warren (on the course CD)*

So John takes us back to before the beginning; before the beginning of time itself. Christ, John tells us, was 'in the beginning with God'. Indeed, Christ was not just with God, he was and *is* God.

Where the earlier gospel writers had focused on the *humanity* of the Babe of Bethlehem, John explores and opens up for us the divinity of Christ. Here is the astonishing claim: that the One who brought all that is into existence is the One who came as a child in a manger, and was later to die on a Roman cross.

To grasp the significance of who the child of Bethlehem was is quite mind-blowing. But more than this, it should stir us to join the song of the angels praising God and saying, *'glory to God in the highest and on earth peace among those whom he favours'* (Luke 2.14). This is the One whom we worship today. Truly to grasp this would make us less inclined, when we pray, to rush in with our list of requests. Rather, starting our praying by giving worship – that is, paying loving attention to God – gives us the right perspective on our requests.

The source of life and light

John 1.4-5: John now delves more deeply into the work of creation. It was not just the bringing into being of what we call the 'natural order' of galaxies, stars and planets with their teeming and myriad forms of life. There was something deeper going on. John highlights that creation by using three telling phrases. Each phrase has a key word – **life, light**

and **darkness** – not just central in creation but a vital theme in the whole of the gospel that follows:

[a] *'In him was life'* (v 4). The word 'life' is used more than thirty times in this gospel, for example:

- *'I came that they might have life, and have it abundantly'* (10.10)
- *'God so loved the world that he gave his only Son, so that everyone who believes in him may not perish but have eternal life'* (3.16)
- *'These are written that you may believe that Jesus is the Messiah, the Son of God, and that through believing you may have life in his name'* (20.31)

This life is not mere existence. It is a special quality of life: eternal life. That is not about endless existence starting when we die, but about a new quality of life that begins when we believe. Eternal life is essentially the life of the Age to Come – the life of heaven – breaking into our here-and-now. This is what the coming of Christ brings into this world: a new level of life energised by access to the source of life, namely God himself. It is life lived in awareness, and under the life-giving guidance, of the One who comes to us in the whole of life – its joys and its dark times.

"When in doubt, mumble; when in trouble, delegate; when in charge, ponder."

James H. Boren, American writer

[b] *'The life was the **light** of all people'* (v.4). John used the word 'light' more than twenty times, as in:

- *'I am the light of the world. Whoever follows me will never walk in darkness but will have the light of life'* (8.12)
- *'while you have the light, believe in the light, so that you may become children of the light'* (12.36)

How different the countryside looks when the sun breaks through. It is that sort of difference when the light of Christ shines on, and into, our lives. We see things differently. We marvel at the beauty and generosity of life, and the God who gives life. We see our part in that world in a clearer light when we open ourselves to the One who comes.

[c] Darkness

- *'The darkness did not overcome it'* (v.5).
- *'the light has come into the world and people loved darkness rather than light'* (3.19)
- About Judas' betrayal: *'after receiving the piece of bread, he immediately went out. And it was night'* (13.30)

It is striking that in the opening verses of the gospel, which celebrate the wonder of the Christ who came to this world, John should recognise the reality of darkness too. There are some forms of Christian spirituality that only ever want to be positive and say nice things. It is well-meaning but not true spirituality. Christian spirituality can face the dark, for Christ is the One who came to uncover, and overcome, the darkness in us and in our world. Christian spirituality has been described rather as 'hippopotamus spirituality' – resources for surviving in the mud!

Preparing the Way

John 1.6-9: John has begun his gospel with the focus on the wonder of the Word-made-flesh. Now, as with Luke, he roots the story of Christ's coming in historical events, namely the ministry of John the Baptist.

> "I think our contemporary society doesn't leave much room for pondering. I think by nature I'm quite a slow, thinking person, and I like to think that that gets me somewhere. Quite where, I don't know!"
>
> *Andrew (on the course CD)*

All four Gospel writers introduce John the Baptist as the one who prepares the way for the coming of Christ. The image of preparing the way comes from a scripture set in the far off days when the Israelites were in exile in Babylon. God used the secular king Cyrus to make possible their return to the Promised Land. The image in Isaiah (40.3-5) is that of preparing for a royal visitor. Everything must be made ready. It is like the building of new motorways with valleys levelled, hills cut through and the roads straightened out.

This is the work of the Holy Spirit – though human agencies are frequently involved. Many of us can point to those who have guided us towards faith in Christ, and along the Way of following him. We may even play this role in the lives of others, though we will often be unaware that we have done so.

St Augustine, in his classic book, *Confessions*, identified two such pointers in his journey to faith. First was his mother, Monica, who had prayed for him, and no doubt pointed him to Christ by the way she lived and the way she loved him. Secondly, Augustine saw some unknown children playing. He thought they were shouting out, 'take up and read'. This prompted him to 'take up and read' the scriptures he had with him. Augustine came to yield his life to the One who came to him as he read those scriptures.

For us to be someone who points the way for others, like Jesus and John the Baptist, we need to co-operate with God's work in us. That co-operation involves our allowing God to bring about changes in our lives that will make a way in our wildernesses for the coming of the King of Kings.

Receiving Christ

John 1.10-13: So far, we have looked at the way in which the coming of Christ calls us both to wonder and ponder at that event, in both its past and present impacts. But there is a further step by which Christian spirituality finds expression as a response to the coming of Christ. It is the step of *receiving* Christ – opening ourselves to him.

The coming of Christ is, as John says, like the coming of light. Christ, the light of the world, uncovers dark areas in our lives. Jesus takes no delight in 'finding us out', but he does delight in 'calling us out' – out of our darkness and into the light of truth, beauty, goodness and love of God.

John identifies *receiving* as the key to walking God's way. Bringing our lives before God and looking to Christ to direct our choices, priorities and attitudes in life are all part of receiving Christ. It is not just a 'once in a lifetime' step, it is how we walk in the Way of Christ. Our culture, however, teaches us that being in control of our own life is the ultimate sign of maturity.

Back to pondering

There is a rhythm and a pattern to following Christ. Yes, the right starting points are in stopping the rush of life long enough to give God our worship (which is what *wonder* is about) and to listen to what God has to say to us (which is what it means to *ponder*).

That then leads on to *receiving* grace, and *reflecting* that in the way we live our lives.

> "Were there no God, we would be in this glorious world with grateful hearts: and no one to thank."
>
> *Christina Rossetti, poet*

John is eager to get into the story of the ministry of Christ, about which he has so much to say. But before he does so, he pauses – and reflects further on what it is about Christ that he has seen, and longs for others to see. Two things stand out.

First, John has seen, and been overwhelmed and energised by, grace and truth in all their fullness. *'From his fullness have we all received, grace upon grace'* (v.16). Grace is generous, undeserved goodness. It comes from God who is goodness, generosity and grace personified.

Second, John has seen something particular about how *'the Word was with God'* (v.1). It is in the depth and quality of relationship between the Father and the Son (vv14,18). There is a divine intimacy that makes them one, so that Jesus can say to Philip, *'whoever has seen me has seen the Father'* (14.9).

Here is something very special that John will spell out in due course. It is what the believer receives: namely, the same intimacy with God, as there is between Father and Son. John Chapter 15 uses the vivid imagery of the vine and branches to explore this most glorious of gifts. It is open to all of us who will stop long enough to ponder these things and to receive their truths into our lives.

QUESTIONS FOR GROUPS

1. John uses words about Jesus such as life, light, grace, truth. What words would you use to describe Jesus to someone today?

2. Some people, when they come to God in personal prayer, use a verse from scripture or a hymn, to focus their thoughts on God. Do you have a favourite way of 'paying loving attention to God'?

3. Have you seen the light and life of Christ making a difference in some way in the life of someone you know, or know of?

4. John the Baptist is described as someone 'sent from God'. Have you ever felt, or seen in others, a sense of God calling you to do something – and what was it? Did you feel able to respond?

5. **Track 20 on the CD/Transcript.** What's the difference between a wicked act and an evil act?

6. What would help you, personally and as a church, to ponder about God? Books, sermons, courses … or something else?

7. Here are three quotes about the dark. How do they help you face the dark places and dark times in life – if they do?

    •   'Darkness cannot drive out darkness: only light can do that. Hate cannot drive out hate: only love can do that.' (*Martin Luther King Jr*)

    •   'We can easily forgive a child who is afraid of the dark; the real tragedy of life is when adults are afraid of the light.' (*Plato*)

    •   'Look how a single candle can both defy and define the darkness.' (*Anne Frank*)

8. Theologian Rudolph Bultmann defined sin as 'our determination to manage by ourselves'. Robert Warren writes, on p. 14 'Our culture teaches us that being in control of our own life is the ultimate sign of maturity.' Do you feel that you need to retain some control – or do you have to turn it all over to God? And if the latter, how do you do this?

9. **Read Philippians 4.8-9.** Thinking of the matter of pondering, what practical steps do you, or can you, take to 'think on these things?'

10. Choose one of the quote boxes that you might like to discuss.

Receiving: Mary's response to the coming of Christ

Luke 1.39-55

[39]*In those days Mary set out and went with haste to a Judean town in the hill country,* [40]*where she entered the house of Zechariah and greeted Elizabeth.* [41]*When Elizabeth heard Mary's greeting, the child leapt in her womb. And Elizabeth was filled with the Holy Spirit* [42]*and exclaimed with a loud cry, 'Blessed are you among women, and blessed is the fruit of your womb.* [43]*And why has this happened to me, that the mother of my Lord comes to me?* [44]*For as soon as I heard the sound of your greeting, the child in my womb leapt for joy.* [45]*And blessed is she who believed that there would be a fulfilment of what was spoken to her by the Lord.'*

[46]*And Mary said,*
'My soul magnifies the Lord,
[47]*and my spirit rejoices in God my Saviour,*
[48]*for he has looked with favour on the lowliness of his servant.*
Surely, from now on all generations will call me blessed;
[49]*for the Mighty One has done great things for me, and holy is his name.*
[50]*His mercy is for those who fear him from generation to generation.*
[51]*He has shown strength with his arm;*
he has scattered the proud in the thoughts of their hearts.
[52]*He has brought down the powerful from their thrones, and lifted up the lowly;*
[53]*he has filled the hungry with good things, and sent the rich away empty.*
[54]*He has helped his servant Israel, in remembrance of his mercy,*
[55]*according to the promise he made to our ancestors,*
to Abraham and to his descendants for ever.'

The story of the visit of Mary to her cousin Elizabeth, and the song of Mary which follows (1.46-55), is the earliest and most personal of the four events that this course explores. For Mary, the coming has already taken place. Christ is conceived within her. She – and indeed, Elizabeth too – is now responding to that mystifying event.

This seemingly innocent little incident, about two pregnant cousins 'having a natter', is itself

> "Getters don't get – givers get."
>
> *Eugene Benge, writer*

pregnant with insights about how we are to respond to the coming of Christ in our own lives. Mary and Elizabeth, by their responses, point us to: three things: openness to God in the whole of life; two-way honesty and care; the cost of blessing.

> "Until we can receive with an open heart, we're never really giving with an open heart. When we attach judgment to receiving help, we knowingly or unknowingly attach judgment to giving help."
>
> *Brené Brown, scholar and author*

1. Openness to God in the whole of life

Mary is responding to Gabriel's message. Whether she had immediately told Joseph or was wanting to talk it over first with Elizabeth we do not know. What we do know is that she needed the understanding, support and help of Elizabeth. As Mary greeted her, Elizabeth was just as quick to own her own need to share that her child had moved in her womb – and the significance she attached to that.

This 'owning our feelings' seems quite modern, although it has always been part of what it means to be human. Too easily nowadays, owning our feelings can lead us then to feed on them, hugging them to ourselves and using them to put ourselves centre-stage. For Mary and Elizabeth, their feelings and reactions prompted them to be open to each other, and to the presence of God in their situation. As a result they ended up being open to God, to each other and to life.

Our culture teaches us that our goal in life should be to 'take control' of it. Mary and Elizabeth point to a counter-intuitive response: to loosen our grip and to open up to the generosity, presence and love that come from God. In doing so they discovered, as we do too, that God, in humility, often chooses to do his work through other people. Roberta Bondi wrote in *To Love as God Loves*: *'Only as we learn to love God and others do we gain real freedom and autonomy in a society in which most people live in a state of slavery to their needs and desires'.*

2. Two-way honesty and care

There is, without a doubt, a place for professional counselling from those who have been trained and have a lifetime of experience; but love knows nothing of the provider/client relationship. Love is a deep sharing of openness, and so of blessing. This is the hallmark of 'Christian community': honesty, a shared openness to bless and be blessed, and an abiding awareness of God in it all. In such encounters one can never predict who might most fully encounter God and be enriched in the human exchange!

However, in seeking to 'bless' it is important to steer clear of any sentimentality. God's blessing is always part of the divine call and equips us to share in the work of the kingdom: overcoming evil with good; bringing everything into the wholeness of God's loving purposes. For such a task we need courage and integrity to face hard truths and costly decisions about God's call on our lives. Jesus highlights the danger

> "And there's also 'To him that hath shall be given.' After all, you must have a capacity to receive, or even omnipotence can't give. Perhaps your own passion temporarily destroys the capacity."
>
> *C S Lewis*

of a sentimental spirituality in Luke 11.27-28: *While he was saying this, a woman in the crowd raised her voice and said to him, 'Blessed is the womb that bore you and the breasts that nursed you!' But he said, 'Blessed rather are those who hear the word of God and obey it!'*

3. The cost of blessing

The Scottish Presbyterian bible scholar, William Barclay, wrote: *'Nowhere better can we see the paradox of blessedness than in the life of Mary.'*

To learn that we are loved, chosen and blessed by God is a profoundly enriching discovery. However, when we sense God's call it doesn't necessarily make life plain sailing. God doesn't come to make life easy. God comes to make us whole. Getting there can be painful and costly. Our problem often is that we're not as eager to be whole people as God is to lead us down that path!

Mary will learn from Simeon something of the mystery and cost of choosing God's way:

Then Simeon blessed them and said to his mother Mary:
this child is destined for the falling and rising of many in Israel,
and to be a sign that will be opposed,
so that the inner thoughts of many will be revealed
and a sword will pierce your own soul too.
(Luke 2.34-35)

The apostle Paul expressed graphically the cost to him of responding to the call of God, in his heartfelt testimony in 1 Corinthians 4.1-13, which he tellingly summarises by saying, *'death is at work in us, but life in you'* (2 Corinthians 4.12).

Making the heart sing

Despite the challenges and cost of responding to the call of God, it is often those moments that prove to be windows into heaven.

Luke, alone among the gospel writers, records a number of songs of praise to God in the course of his story of the birth of Christ. They come from the lips of Mary, Zachariah and Simeon. But there is another one – hidden here in this text. It is the first of all these songs, on the lips of Elizabeth – brief, yet deeply poetic in nature:

'Blessed are you among women, and blessed is the fruit of your womb.
And why has this happened to me, that the mother of my Lord comes to me?
For as soon as I heard the sound of your greeting,
the child in my womb leapt for joy.
And blessed is she who believed
that there would be a fulfilment of what was spoken to her by the Lord.' (1.42-45)

Christian spirituality – responding to the coming of Christ – turns our focus onto God rather than ourselves. Being open to God, to other people, and to life itself leads us to experience grace, mercy and insight. It calls out of us the response of faith that leads us to worship – and of worship that strengthens our faith.

Mary's Song

Luke 1.46-48: Not surprisingly, Mary starts by giving thanks to God for his goodness to her. It is a good way for us to begin our praying – better than starting by asking. Our first task in prayer is to orientate ourselves in God's presence and connect with the great unseen reality of God in our lives and in the world. Doing so puts our requests into perspective.

Mary praises God for noticing someone who feels insignificant – as we all can feel at times. She speaks of her *'lowliness as a servant of God'* (v.48). However, although this is her starting point, she does not focus on herself, but on God. She calls God her *Lord* (v.46), *Saviour* (v.47) *Mighty*

> "My experience as a pastor is that, when I go to pastor somebody with a problem, I can never be sure who's going to be most blessed at the end of this encounter. It may well be me, rather than them."
>
> *Canon Robert Warren*
> *(on the course CD)*

One (v.49) and she calls God *holy* (v.49) and the one who has brought her blessing or significance. Her attention is on God. She is mulling over God's nature. For us too, simply stopping, being quiet and naming some names of God *(Shepherd, Rock, Delight,* etc.), then thanking God for the gift of life and the joy of living, is a good way to start any 'prayer time'.

Luke 1.50: Mary's praise broadens out beyond her own experience as she reflects on the experience of the people of God down many centuries. She sums up the overarching nature of God's dealings with his people by calling God a God of mercy.

Luke 1.51-52: Mary now steps out beyond her own life, and the life of the people of God. She looks out to the far horizons of her knowledge of the world and delights that God is not only a God of *mercy*, but a God of *justice* too. As such, God is in the business of righting wrongs and dealing with oppressors of every sort. Despite so much conflict, injustice and oppression, we can see good overcoming evil throughout the ages. Think of Nazism in Germany, Pol Pot in Thailand, and – on a different level – the current fight to eradicate malaria. We can give thanks that, as John put it, *'the light shines in the darkness, and the darkness did not overcome it'* (John 1.5). Evil has an uncanny way of destroying itself, even if only after much suffering has been brought to many. Mary sees how her personal experience of God is reflected in God's dealings with the nations.

As a hymn by Arthur Campbell reminds us:

God is working His purpose out
as year succeeds to year;
God is working his purpose out,
and the time is drawing near;
nearer and nearer draws the time,
the time that shall surely be,
when the earth shall be filled
with the glory of God
as the waters cover the sea.

Luke 1.52-55: At the end of her Song of Praise, like a ship righting itself in the waves, Mary's attention returns to God. A safe anchorage is reached in the steadfast love of God. This is the harbour from which her song set out. Praise, petition and pondering on the character of God, and God's actions in our troubled world, have all been expressed in these nine verses. Being still before God, in silent adoration and thanksgiving, is a good way not just to begin, but also to end time before God.

The Advent Hope

The tenses of the verbs in this Song of Mary are interesting. They are all past tenses, yet the job of righting the wrongs of the world is clearly not complete. The past tense is being used here to express confidence in what is yet to come. Here we glimpse the heart of the Advent Hope: the final coming of God's kingdom.

The D-Day Landings in World War II have been used to illustrate hope. Those successful landings, and the bridgeheads they established, were not the end – but they were the beginning of the end. The End could now be glimpsed, though much suffering still lay ahead. So too with the coming of Christ. A bridgehead has been established. The End is in sight to the eye of faith.

'Hope' is popularly used to describe little more than wishful thinking, as in 'I hope my team will win the Cup this year', or 'I hope it will be sunny this weekend!' 'Hope', as used in the Bible, has a much stronger meaning. It describes something we are *confident* will happen in the future (Hebrews 6.11). It is this confidence in God's purposes for the future that has sustained the saints in the most testing of times. It was this sort of hope that sustained William Wilberforce and his supporters for over 40 years to get the Abolition of Slavery onto the Statute Books. This is what Hope is ultimately about: confidence that, in the End, good will triumph over evil.

There is a further dimension to the Advent Hope. Many churches, in the Eucharist, administer the bread and wine with such words as 'the body/ blood of Christ keep you in eternal life'. 'Eternal life', as noted in the last session, means 'life of the New Age', or 'Life of the Age to Come'. God's call to us, and God's gift to us, is to enable us now to live the life that will find ultimate expression in heaven. It is this that gives hope, purpose, direction and confidence in the journey of faith. We do not have to wait until death to live in the presence of God. Jesus comes to us here and now.

QUESTIONS FOR GROUPS

1. **Track 33 on the CD/Transcript.** Mary and Elizabeth were able to be real, honest and supportive of each other. Can you recall a time when you have had an experience like that? What might help you, and others, to experience such times in the future? Do you feel that men and women are equally good at being mutually honest and supportive? (No fighting!)

2. **Track 38 on the CD/Transcript.** What makes your heart sing? On a low day is there a memory /place /reading /song /hymn ... you can turn to that you know will lift your spirits?

3. On p. 19 Robert Warren writes that 'Evil has an uncanny way of destroying itself, even if only after much suffering has been brought to many.' Do you agree?

4. Re-read the final paragraph of p. 20. The Advent Hope is about God's ultimate purposes for all creation. Nobel prize-winning climatologist Sir John Houghton has talked about having confidence in God's covenant with his people that God won't let us down over climate change. Are you as confident that God has everything under control?

5. **Track 37 on the CD/Transcript. Read Luke 1.46-55.** There is a clear structure to Mary's Song with its heartfelt personal thanksgiving and worship; prayer for a troubled world; quiet reliance and resting in the goodness of God. Might this be a helpful pattern for your prayers? Are there other patterns that help you that you can share?

6. In his book *Love over Scotland*, Alexander McCall Smith wrote: "*Gracious acceptance is an art – an art which most never bother to cultivate. We think that we have to learn how to give, but we forget about accepting things, which can be much harder than giving ... Accepting another person's gift is allowing him to express his feelings for you.*" What has life taught you about receiving? Have you ever struggled to accept an apology from someone who has hurt you?

7. On p. 18 Robert Warren writes, 'God doesn't come to make life easy.' But why not?

8. On p. 20 Robert writes: 'This is what Hope is ultimately about: confidence that, in the End, good will triumph over evil.' Do you share Robert's confidence?

9. **Track 29 on the CD/Transcript.** St Augustine said that, 'God gives where he finds empty hands.' Too easily our response to God is to say, in effect, 'I'm sorry but I have got my hands full at the moment.' How might you set about emptying your hands – making more room for God?

10. Can you recall or identify some skill you have developed over the years, or some change of attitude you have embraced? How did that happen? What does that have to say about 'receiving Christ'?

Living: Paul rejoices in the coming of Christ

Philippians 2.5-11

⁵*Let the same mind be in you that was in Christ Jesus,*
⁶*who, though he was in the form of God,*
did not regard equality with God as something to be exploited,
⁷*but emptied himself, taking the form of a slave, being born in human likeness.*
And being found in human form,
⁸*he humbled himself and became obedient to the point of death— even death on a cross.*
⁹*Therefore God also highly exalted him and gave him the name that is above every name,*
¹⁰*so that at the name of Jesus every knee should bend,*
in heaven and on earth and under the earth,
¹¹*and every tongue should confess that Jesus Christ is Lord, to the glory of God the Father.*

William Barclay once said of Philippians 2.5-11: 'This is the greatest and most moving passage Paul ever wrote about Jesus.' In this final session we will be exploring this remarkable, indeed unique, passage in the New Testament. It is a hymn – whether written by Paul or not, we do not know – based on an Aramaic original. Aramaic was the language of Jesus and the disciples, so this hymn comes from the very earliest days of the faith. But it is more than a hymn; it is also a brief life story of Jesus and a creed, as well as a pattern for living.

As we have seen, Matthew's Gospel traced Jesus' ancestry back to Abraham; Luke's Gospel traced it further back to Adam; and John's Gospel traced Jesus' origins right back to before the beginning of time when *'the Word was with God and Word was God'.*

> '*Siyahamba ekukhanyeni kwenkos yoyo*'
> ('We are marching in the light of God')
> *Zulu folk song/hymn*

Now Paul completes the story of the child of Bethlehem by taking us forward, beyond his birth, to his ministry and death, then on to his resurrection, ascension and exaltation to 'the right hand of God'. We now see the story of Jesus from beginning to end; though, in truth, there was no beginning and there will be no end.

This comprehensive overview comes as part of Paul's encouragement of the Christians in Philippi to become a loving community. He highlights Christ's willingness to lay aside his glory in order to give expression to God's love for all. Paul sees the Philippians needing to face the same call to choose God's way: 'have this mind among you' (Philippians 2.5). This following of Christ is our calling too.

Paul calls us to respond to the coming of Christ by living as Christ lived. So, what is involved in living as Christ lived? To find out, we'll divide this hymn into two parts: verses 5-8 and then verses 9-11.

'He laid aside His majesty' (Philippians 2.5-8)

One of the constant themes of Paul's teaching about Jesus is expressed well in 2 Corinthians 8.9: *'though he was rich, yet for your sakes he became poor, so that by his poverty you might become rich'*.

Turning to the first part of our passage, Philippians 2.5-8, we discover it begins with Jesus laying aside the glory of heaven. This 'letting go' and humility are continued in his earthly life by Jesus *'taking the form of a slave'*, living out of obedience to the Father.

This obedience is not through force or coercion. Its motivation is love – in two ways:

● First, Jesus is motivated by his response to the Father's 'steadfast love' for creation. Jesus freely chose to embrace the life-giving purposes of the Father. Choosing the will of his Father shaped the whole of Jesus' living. In prayer, he sought to discover the will of his Father. Having discerned what that was, he freely chose to act

upon it. It is this approach to life that sustained Jesus: *'My food is to do the will of him who sent me and to complete his work.'* (John 4.34.)

● Second, Jesus is motivated by his response to the brokenness of humanity. Jesus did not cling to the power and glory that were his 'by right'. Love caused him to set all that aside for us. It is like someone who, seeing a person being swept away by a strong current, sheds their clothes and dives in to rescue them. The issue in the mind of such a person is not, 'What's in this for me?' but rather, 'What can I do to help?'

The dominant theme in this part of the hymn is that of Jesus choosing, freely, to discover and to do the will of the Father. And the will of the Father is to express steadfast love and blessing to all creation. Just as Jesus worked alongside Joseph in the carpenter's shop, so, in his ministry Jesus worked with God the Father to fulfil God's purposes of love. Jesus

> "When people say 'Charity begins at home' they very often mean 'You should look after your own kids, family and own circle first and then be kind to people' which is not the original meaning of the proverb. The original meaning is that charity begins in the home – that is to say kids learn charity in the home."
>
> *Hugh MacKay, writer*

described his work on earth in these terms: *'the Son can do nothing on his own, but only what he sees the Father doing; for whatever the Father does, the Son does likewise.'* (John 5.19.)

'The Name above all names' (Philippians 2.9-11)

The second part of this hymn describes what we might call 'the upward arc' of the journey of Jesus. This takes us through his resurrection and ascension on to his exaltation at the right hand of God. Here the dynamic shifts from Jesus *'choosing'* to the Father *'exalting'*. Jesus is raised by his Father from the dead, seated at his own right hand, and given a new name.

At first glance this 'new name' appears to be 'Jesus' (v.10). The name once placarded on the Cross is now exalted in highest heaven. This is wonderfully expressed in Charles Wesley's great hymn:

Jesus the name high over all,
Jesus, the name to sinners dear,
In hell, or earth, or sky:
The name to sinners giv'n

Angels and men before it fall,
It scatters all their guilty fear,
And devils fear and fly.
It brings them peace of heav'n

However, on closer inspection, the new name that is given is that of 'Lord'. The honour that had only ever been given to God the Father is now given to Jesus, to whom *'every tongue [will] confess that Jesus Christ is Lord'* (v.11).

Motivation

Jesus was never chasing personal honour and glory. His only motivations were the rightness of his Father's way, and the needs of broken humanity. So too for the Christian. Doing what is right, what God calls us to, is its own reward. As the prayer of St Ignatius puts it: *'not to ask for any reward, save that of knowing that I do your will'.*

However, this exaltation is not the end of the story of Christ. He is honoured with the title 'Lord'; and at that very point his ultimate motivation is revealed. He acted, and always acts, 'to the glory of God the Father'. Jesus gives glory to the Father, the source of all goodness, honour and love. No wonder the prayer he taught his disciples to pray begins *'Our Father in heaven, your name be hallowed'.*

Jesus Christ is Lord

The phrase, 'Jesus Christ is Lord', became the Church's earliest creed. It brought the Church into conflict with Rome, for Caesar also had the

> "In the end what matters is not how good we are but how good God is. Not how much we love Him but how much He loves us. And God loves us whoever we are, whatever we've done or failed to do, whatever we believe or can't."
>
> *Archbishop Desmond Tutu*

> "It's quite clear from the New Testament that the one thing people remembered about Jesus' own prayers and about his teaching on prayer was that he called God 'Father'. He used the familiar word 'Abba,' the intimate word for 'father' in his own language. So the first thing that Jesus says when he talks to God is 'Father'. He doesn't call God 'Creator' or 'Lord' or 'Master', he says 'Father'. The first word he says affirms his relationship with God."
>
> *Archbishop Rowan Williams and Sr Wendy Beckett in their book*
> Living the Lord's Prayer

title 'Lord' thereby asserting the Emperor's divinity. What bound the empire together was that all citizens were required to offer sacrifice to Caesar as Lord as an act of worship. Christians refused to do so, saying that only Jesus should receive that title. Persecution and martyrdom were the price they paid.

This creed expressed a vision of God's care and involvement in the whole of human life, and the shaping of society and its values and goals. In the earliest centuries the Church became virtually the welfare arm of the Roman Empire. In succeeding centuries, hospitals and schools were set up first by the Church.

In the British Isles, the revival under John Wesley had a major impact on society, including the overcoming of widespread alcohol addiction among the poor. It was also Wesley who, looking for a Christian form of sport to replace bear-baiting, introduced football! In the nineteenth-century, prison reform (Elizabeth Fry), the development of

nursing (Florence Nightingale) and the establishing of Trade Unions to speak for workers, all emerged as a result of Christian initiatives.

In our own times initiatives in famine relief and development agencies have been and still are much influenced by Christians and Christian values; as have been the founding of Alcoholics Anonymous, Telephone Samaritans and the Hospice Movement.

The vision of God's loving purposes in the world, arising from the conviction that 'Jesus Christ is Lord', has had a major impact for good throughout the whole Christian era.

Responding to the coming of Christ

In the introduction to this course, we defined Christian spirituality as 'our response to the coming of Christ'. Over the sessions we have noted four particular aspects of that response, namely: *wonder, pondering, receiving* and *living*. So we conclude this course by thinking about how

> "We hear of the Spirit who fills his people with love and joy and peace, but hear less of the Spirit who sometimes leads his people as he led Jesus into the wilderness, where they can face weakness, pain, failure rather than run away from them."
>
> *Canon John Holmes*

we give expression to these characteristics of Christian spirituality.

Wondering: A good indication that we have grasped the wonder of the coming of Christ, into this world and into our lives, is the extent of our desire to worship God. Worship is rather like a blind person finding their way. It is not God who needs our worship, but we ourselves who need to worship God, in order to find our way. It brings to our attention the unseen reality of the greatness, goodness and nearness of God, and centres our existence on him, not on ourselves.

Three of the four passages studied during this course include worship: the angels' heavenly praises at the birth of Christ; Mary's song of praise; and, in this session, a hymn from the early Church's worship of God. The third passage, John Chapter 1, is very close to worship too. The hymn we've been exploring in this fourth session is the result of meditation, prayer and worship.

Pondering, as Mary did, involves meditation, prayer and worship. Each of the scriptures this course has explored is, quite evidently, the fruit of profound and fertile reflection.

Jesus washing the disciples' feet, recorded in John 13.1-20, is a specific act that expresses what Paul is saying in Philippians 2.6-11. Just as Jesus laid aside the glory of heaven, here he lays aside his outer clothing. He leads by serving the needs of his disciples, rather than by 'lording' it over them. He shocks them by the extent to which he will give himself to bring life to others.

Making time to meditate on the scriptures, and on any prayer to God that arises from that, is the best way to be well grounded in the faith. It enables us to find our rightful place in the world, and to discover our particular calling in life.

R A Torrey, the great 19th/20th century American evangelist, pastor, and educator, wrote this: *'Prayer that is born of meditation upon the Word of God is the prayer that soars upward most easily to God's listening ears.'*

Receiving: Paul points us to ways in which we are to receive Christ (Philippians 2.5-11). It is to let Christ's whole approach to life be the pattern for our living. *'Let the same mind be in you that was in Christ Jesus.'* Paul calls us to receive Christ's attitude to life and to let it shape the way we handle our living. This involves joining in with God's

> "For me, God is the ultimate mind-like reality behind the universe which wants every sentient being to have a life of joy and happiness for eternity. That's my view of God."
>
> *Professor Keith Ward speaking on York Courses'* Why I believe in God *CD*

purposes in our lives and the world around us, choosing to be yoked to Jesus and share his approach to life. (Matthew 11.28-30.)

The Christian life is not to be lived in our own, very limited, strength, but by the grace we receive from God. Paul speaks of Christ living in us and testifies that, *'I toil and struggle with all the energy he powerfully inspires within me'* (Colossians 1.29).

One way we can draw upon God's strength to live as Jesus calls us to, is to shift from *anxious pleading* for God's help to *joyful thanksgiving* for what God has already promised. So, rather than an attitude of 'please, please God give me peace' when we feel our lack, we simply need to open our hands, hearts and lives to receive what God longs for us to have. In doing so it is good to remember, as St Augustine put it,

that 'God gives where he finds open hands'. Better by far to pray: 'thank you for the promise of your peace. I receive it right now, by faith.' (Matthew 21.22.)

Living: The end of all faith in God is the pursuit of his purposes of love in our daily living. This is to live responsively to God's will and guidance. It is living in the light of the coming of Christ.

Rather than being *driven* by the urge to achieve, control, possess or simply own things, the Christian is to choose to listen to the still small voice of God, and to live out of a sense of *vocation*. The call of God is to all believers and for the whole of life. Paul summarises that calling in these words: *'Do not be overcome by evil, but overcome evil with good.'* (Romans 12.21.)

> "How wonderful it is that nobody need wait a single moment before starting to improve the world!"
>
> *Anne Frank, diarist and Holocaust victim*

QUESTIONS FOR GROUPS

1. Someone who is not a church-goer asks you, 'So what's so special about Jesus?' How, in the light of Philippians 2.6-11, would you reply?

2. If we do good things, and are kind, but do them for selfish reasons of our own – does this actually matter? **Track 44 of the CD/Transcript might help.**

3. This course has tried to see worship as *wonder*? Does this make sense to you? Have you ever experienced worship as wonder?

4. Is there any particular insight you have had as a result of paying attention to the *pondering* of Luke, John, Mary or Paul? Has it motivated or helped you with your own reflecting on the ways in which God comes to us?

5. Are there ways in which this course has helped you see *receiving from Jesus* in a new light? If so, does that help you to understand worship in a new or different way?

6. **Track 43 of the CD/Transcript.** 'Charity begins at home' is an old (and perhaps mis-used) adage. Do you see the life of Jesus underlining that, giving you a new perspective on it, or … ?

7. What stops you, in your daily *living*, from following Jesus' approach more fully? Are there practical things we could all do to support one another in removing any obstacles to being closer followers?

8. Re-read the first question of Session One on p. 9. How did you answer that question? How accurate were your predictions? Have these sessions changed how you see 'Bible Study' and if so, in what way?

9. Choose one aspect of Christ's nature (e.g. compassion, generosity) and think about how you might work on improving this quality in yourself and/or in your church.

10. Look ahead. What is the future for your group? Meet again? Another course perhaps? (See the facing page for some ideas!) Perhaps hold a social event (a coffee morning maybe) and invite others to join you?

You may like to finish with a closing prayer, such as:

> *Eternal God,*
> *the light of the minds that know you,*
> *the joy of the hearts that love you,*
> *and the strength of the wills that serve you:*
> *grant us so to know you*
> *that we may truly love you,*
> *so to love you that we may truly serve you,*
> *whose service is perfect freedom;*
> *through Jesus Christ our Lord.*
>
> after Augustine of Hippo (430AD)